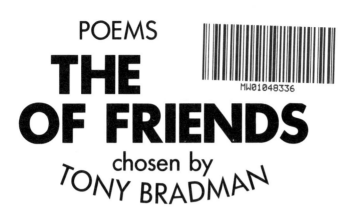

POEMS
THE
OF FRIENDS
chosen by
TONY BRADMAN

Illustrated by Madeleine Baker

BLACKIE

British Library Cataloguing in Publication Data

Bradman, Tony, *1954–*
The best of friends.
I. Title   II. Baker, Madeleine
821'.914
ISBN 0-216-92330-1

Blackie and Son Ltd
7 Leicester Place
London WC2H 7BP

Typeset by Jamesway Graphics, Middleton, Manchester
Printed in Great Britain by Thomson Litho Ltd, East Kilbride, Scotland.

Turn these pages and you'll see
How important friends can be.
Friends who make for happy days,
Who can be fun in lots of ways;
Friends whose friendship never fails,
Friends who show off, friends with tails;
Friends who make you feel all right,
And friends who only want to fight.
Friends who leave you on your own,
And those you talk to on the phone . . .
Friends at school, and some outside,
Friends in whom you can confide,
Friends who hardly seem to care,
And one or two who just aren't there.
So long before you reach the end
You'll know about the best of friends . . .

Let's Talk

Lips are for speaking
And smiling too.
Tongues are for saying
How do you do?

Hands are for waving
To people on the street
And hearts are for loving
Everyone we meet.

Ask the person on your left
If he would be your friend
Then turn to your right
And do the same again.

Telcine Turner

Puzzle

My best friend's name is Billy
But his best friend is Fred
And Fred's is Willy Wiffleson
And Willy's best is Ted.
Ted's best pal is Samuel
While Samuel's is Paul . . .
It's funny Paul says I'm his best —
I hate him most of all.

Arnold Spilka

7

Best Friends

It's Susan I talk to not Tracey,
Before that I sat next to Jane;
I used to be best friends with Lynda
But these days I think she's a pain.

Natasha's all right in small doses,
I meet Mandy sometimes in town;
I'm jealous of Annabel's pony
And I don't like Nicola's frown.

I used to go skating with Catherine,
Before that I went there with Ruth;
And Kate's so much better at trampoline:
She's a showoff, to tell you the truth.

I think that I'm going off Susan,
She borrowed my comb yesterday;
I *think* I might sit next to Tracey,
She's my nearly best friend: she's OK.

Adrian Henri

Two Friends

He was a rat, and she was a rat,
  And down in one hole they did dwell;
And both were as black as a witch's cat,
  And they loved one another well.

He had a tail, and she had a tail,
  Both long and curling and fine;
And each said, 'Yours is the finest tail
  In the world, excepting mine.'

Anon

9

The Best of Friends

I'm only little
You're very big
I eat like a little mouse
You eat like a pig

But we're friends, just the same

I like it quiet
You like it LOUD
I like to be alone a lot
You're always in a crowd

But we're friends, just the same

I have seven brothers
You've just got your mum
You're not afraid of anything
I still suck my thumb

But we're friends, just the same

I'm good with numbers
You're good with words
I don't know any funny jokes
Yours are the best I've heard

But we're friends, just the same

10

People say we're different
People call us names
People say we'll never stick together
That our friendship's just a game

But we're friends, just the same

Tony Bradman

A Friendship Poem

There's good mates and bad mates
   'Sorry to keep you waiting' mates
Cheap skates and wet mates
   The ones you end up hating mates
Hard mates and fighting mates
   Witty and exciting mates
Mates you want to hug
   And mates you want to clout
Ones that get you into trouble
   And ones that get you out.

Roger McGough

Confusion

Jean get licks in school today
For hitting Janet Hill
It was just after recess time
And class was playful still
Janet pull Jean ribbon off
And throw it on the ground
Jean got vex and cuff Janet
Same time Miss turn around
Miss didn't ask no questions
She just start beating Jean
Tomorrow Jean mother coming
To fix-up Miss McLean.

Odette Thomas

Lost Battle

I had a fight with a boy
My best friend
And he said to me
That he is going to get his gang
So I ignored him
He came back the same day
With his gang
And they gave me a clobber
So I named it
The lost battle.

Vivian Usherwood

My Best Friend

Johnny Johnson thinks he can run.
Boasts he's the fastest thing under the
    sun;
Says there isn't a race he hasn't won.
But my best friend could beat him.

14

Terry Timpson thinks he can catch.
Boasts he's the star of the cricket match;
Says there isn't a ball that he can't
    snatch.
But my best friend could defeat him.

Big Bill Burton thinks he can fight.
Boasts he's a tiger, morning, noon and
    night;
Says there isn't a kid he can't fright.
But my best friend, Rover, could EAT
    him!

Raymond Wilson

Pussy

Pussy can sit by the fire and sing,
Pussy can climb a tree,
Or play with a silly old cork and string
To 'muse herself, not me.
But I like Binkie my dog, because
He knows how to behave;
So, Binkie's the same as the first Friend
  was,
And I am the Man in the Cave.

Pussy will play Man-Friday till
It's time to wet her paw
And make her walk on the window-sill
(For the footprint Crusoe saw);
Then she fluffles her tail and mews,
And scratches and won't attend.
But Binkie will play whenever I choose,
And he is my true first friend.

16

Pussy will rub my knees with her head
Pretending she loves me hard;
But the very minute I go to bed
Pussy runs out in the yard.
And there she stays till the
    morning-light;
So I know it is only pretend;
But Binkie, he snores at my feet all
    night,
and he is my Firstest Friend!

Rudyard Kipling

Friends

I fear it's very wrong of me,
And yet I must admit,
When someone offers friendship
I want the *whole* of it.
I don't want everybody else
To share my friends with me.
At least, I want *one* special one
Who, indisputably,

Likes me much more than all the rest,
Who's always on my side,
Who never cares what others say,
Who lets me come and hide
Within his shadow, in his house —
It doesn't matter where —
Who lets me simply be myself,
Who's always, *always* there.

Elizabeth Jennings

Since Hanna Moved Away

The tyres on my bike are flat.
The sky is grouchy grey.
At least it sure feels like that
Since Hanna moved away.

Chocolate ice cream tastes like prunes.
December's come to stay.
They've taken back the Mays and Junes
Since Hanna moved away.

Flowers smell like halibut.
Velvet feels like hay.
Every handsome dog's a mutt
Since Hanna moved away.

Nothing's fun to laugh about.
Nothing's fun to play.
They call me, but I won't come out
Since Hanna moved away.

Judith Viorst

Neighbours

The people who live on the right of us
Are very quiet and make no fuss,
But the family on the left clatter about
Day and night, and sometimes shout.

Yet the people on the left of us
Are really rather marvellous,
Instead of being put out by everything
They burst out laughing and sing.
But the family who live on the right of us
Often make me curious,
The way the father whispers to the
mother,
The sister to her silent brother.

I suppose that neighbours are meant
To be different.

Leonard Clark

I Want

I want to be their friend
But they don't want to know me
They say that they are eight years old
And I am only three!

They race on two wheel bikes
But do not notice me
I bet that I could ride one fast
And I am only three.

I want to join their gang
And climb and hide in trees
I know that I can do it too
And I am only three!

I asked, 'Can I join in?'
But they all laughed at me
'Not old enough – just grow up titch'
But I am only three!

Maggie Holmes

Marbles

Hey Jinny, ho Jinny,
what shall we do?
I'm playing marbles —
here are some for you:
Mine has got a ribbon in
green, red, blue.
Hey Jinny, ho Jinny,
Mine has too!

Hey Jinny, ho Jinny
let's have a game —
bowl them and roll them,
there's never two the same!
Some have got a ribbon in
red, green, white,
Hey Jinny, ho Jinny,
aren't they bright?

Hey Jinny, ho Jinny,
lay them in a row:
I'm going to roll one —
it's my go!
Some have got a tassel in
or a bit of twine . . .
Hey Jinny, ho Jinny,
that one's mine!

Jean Kenward

Talking

My friend and I
(Her name's Heather)
Like to talk
When we're together

We talk about playing
We talk about school
We talk about teachers
And stupid school rules

We talk about fathers
We talk about mothers
And brothers and sisters
And sometimes each other

23

We talk about skipping
We talk about walking
We talk about climbing
We talk about *talking*

We talk in the playground
And on our way home
We talk at the gate
And then on the phone

Dad says he wishes
Our talking would end . . .
But what else would *you* do
With your very best friend?

Tony Bradman

Changing

I know what *I* feel like;
I'd like to be *you*
And feel what *you* feel like
And do what *you* do.
I'd like to change places
For maybe a week
And look like your look-alike
And speak as you speak
And think what you're thinking
And go where you go
And feel what you're feeling
And know what you know.
I wish we could do it;
What fun it would be
If I could try you out
And you could try me.

Mary Ann Hoberman

John

John used to be all right.
But he always wanted to fight.
Whenever I went to play,
This is what *I'd* say:
'Let's be brave explorers . . .
That won't bore us!
We can sail in the Pacific,
That would be terrific!
We can bungle through the jungle
And get into a tangle,
But we're friends who never wrangle
However we get mangled.'

And John would say . . . 'Right!
Who do explorers fight?'
Then he'd shout 'ATTACK!'
And jump right on my back.
He would punch and he would bruise
  me . . .

Which is the way to lose me
As someone who's a friend,
Which happened in the end.
For every time I went there
I'd get a finger bent there,
I'd get a scratch or graze
That would hurt for days and days.

So now I play with Tom
Who doesn't fight like John.
He doesn't punch, *he* doesn't bruise . . .
He's a friend I'd hate to lose.

Tony Bradman

I Went Back

I went back after a cold
And nothing was the same.
When the register was called
Even my name
Sounded queer . . . new . . .
(And I was born here too!)
Everyone knew more than me,
Even Kenneth Hannaky
Who's worst usually.
They'd made a play
And puppets from clay
While I was away,
Learnt a song about Cape Horn,
Five guinea pigs were born.
Daffodils in a blue pot
(I planted them)
Bloomed, and I was not
There to see.
Jean had a new coat
And someone, probably George,
Smashed my paper boat.
Monday was a dreadful day.
I wished I was still away.
Tuesday's news day.

I took my stamps to show,
Made a clown called Jo,
Learnt that song from John . . .
Cold's almost gone . . .
And . . . the smallest guinea pig,
Silky black and brown thing,
I'm having
Till Spring.

Gwen Dunn

The Classroom Circle of Friends

and I like Anne
Dan likes me ◆I like Anne
Dee likes Dan Anne likes John
Titch likes Dee John likes Mike
Mo likes Titch Mike likes Ron
Mitch likes Mo Ron likes Paul
Ray likes Mitch Paul likes Pam
Bert likes Ray Pam likes Jack
George likes Bert Jack likes Sam
Gert likes George Sam likes Jane
Jock likes Gert Jane likes Rick
Faye likes Jock Rick likes Jo
Chris likes Faye Jo likes Mick
May likes Chris Mick likes Val
Ken likes May Val likes Jill
Phil likes Ken Jill likes Trish
Trish likes Phil

(◆ start here)
Wes Magee

30

Tracy Venables

Tracy Venables thinks she's great,
Swinging on her garden gate.
She's the girl I love to hate —
'Show-off ' Tracy Venables.

She's so fat she makes me sick,
Eating ice-cream, lick, lick, lick.
I know where I'd like to kick
'Stink-pot' Tracy Venables.

Now she's shouting 'cross the street,
What's she want, the dirty cheat?
Would I like some? Oh, how sweet
Of my friend Tracy Venables.

Colin McNaughton

Write a Poem About a Friend

Hayley is a nice person.
At playtime she is my friend
and during lessons I help her.
She is no good at sums
and can't spell proper.
She has little blue eyes
and she eats too much.
When she yells she goes all red,
her face swells up,
her eyes pop,
and she tells LIES —
like wen she came bak from
play jus now
and sed Im not yore frend no more
yuv a bad temper
i saw what you writ
Well im not yore frend neather
your NASTY Haily!!!

A good start, Justine,
but for some reason
your spelling went off towards the end

Brian Morse

32

I Like You

When you're unkind
You don't mean to be.
And when you're kind
You couldn't care less
Whether or not
You're seen to be.

What I like about you
Is how you know what's cooking
In somebody else's mind.
You do the best you can
And you just don't care
who's looking.

Kit Wright

33

Pictures

Who's your pal?
  It's Michael Perkin,
He's got pictures
  on his jerkin;
he's got pictures
  on his chest —
that's the buddy
  I like best.

Someone's sewn
  for Michael Perkin
spades and buckets
  on his jerkin:
boats and birds
  and bits of sea . . .
I wish they'd make
  the same for me.

I wish—I wish
   I had a jerkin
like the one
   on Michael Perkin,
sewn with pictures
   green and blue.
What has anyone
   made for YOU?

Jean Kenward

I Thought a Lot of You

I thought you were my friend,
I thought you said you'd help;
I thought I could trust you,
I thought I could count on you;
I thought you were loyal,
I thought you would understand;
I thought I'd made it sound
   straightforward,
I thought I had someone to talk to;
I thought you had an answer,
I thought you were a good listener;
I thought I was telling in confidence,
I thought I wasn't being stupid;
I thought you wouldn't make a fool of me,
I thought you weren't going to tell a soul;
     I thought wrong!

P.S. Blackman (Jr)

My Friend Dee

My friend Dee
Is bigger than me,
And I'm more than three feet tall.
My friend Dee
Is bigger than me —
She can see over next-door's wall.

Whenever she looks over,
She laughs and giggles
Or runs and hides
And screams and shivers,
But she *never* tells me
What it is she can see . . .
Of course *I'm* not bothered at all.

Dave Ward

Good Company

I sleep in a room at the top of the house
With a flea, and a fly, and a soft-
    scratching mouse,
And a spider that hangs by a thread from
    the ceiling,
Who gives me each day such a curious
    feeling
When I watch him at work on his
    beautiful weave
Of his web that's so fine I can hardly
    believe
It won't all end up in such terrible
    tangles,
For he sways as he weaves, and spins as
    he dangles,
I cannot get up to that spider, I know,
And hope he won't get down to me here
    below,
And yet when I wake in the chill
    morning air
I'd miss him if he were not still swinging
    there,

For I have in my room such good
    company,
There's him, and the mouse, and the fly,
    and the flea.

Leonard Clark

Just Between You and Me

He's breaking that voice in for somebody
    else
He's borrowed his ears from the
    elephant's graveyard
His brains are as sharp as a squashed
    tomato
His hair has been washed in a bucket of
    lard.

His legs are as straight as strangled
   bananas
His breath smells as sweet as a dead
   skunk's armpit
His nose is so long it touches tomorrow
If he took off his cap his head would go
   with it

His eyes wibble-wobble like glossy fried
   eggs
But he's still my very best friend
Even if his brain was found in a drain
Don't you dare say a word about him—
If I call him names, it's one of our games,
But if you do,
It's rude.

Dave Calder

Mirror Friends

When we look in the mirror,
Me and my friend,
I am brown and she is white.

When we look in the mirror,
Me and my friend,
My hair is dark and hers is light.

And my eyes are black as a raven's wing,
And hers are as blue as a sapphire ring.
She likes chips
And I like rice,
She likes ketchup
And I like spice.

But when we look in the mirror,
Me and my friend,
We feel we are the same as same can be,
Though I am brown and she is white,
We could be sisters,
she and me.

Jamila Gavin

Copycat

Every time we have painting
Jonathan copies me.

Today I did a red house
with a chimney on top,
made smoke come out,
put curtains at the window,
a cat on the doorstep,
a tree in the garden
with one blackbird,
a path, a gate
and a big sun shining.

When I looked at his picture
Jonathan had copied me.

He had a red house,
a smoking chimney,
a cat on the doorstep,
curtains at the window,
a garden, a tree
with a blackbird perched
on the same branch,
a path leading to a gate
and a big sun shining.

The teacher said, 'Which of you copied?'
   but I didn't tell.
Jonathan's a copycat but he's my friend
   as well.

Irene Rawnsley

Imaginary Friends

I have a friend
Who isn't there
In fact she isn't
Anywhere

My friend's imaginary
Or so mum says
And yet I see her
Every day

She sits right next
To me at tea
And also when
I watch TV

She sleeps beside me
In my bed
But my mum says
She's in my head

My friend says
That it's OK
She doesn't mind
What mum says

44

But ssshhh . . . this is secret!
Between you and me
My friend thinks it's *mum*
Who's imaginary!

Tony Bradman

A Boy's Friend

I have a secret friend
With whom I never quarrel.
I'm Watson to his Holmes,
He's Hardy to my Laurel.

I'm greedy for his calls
And leave him with sad heart.
He thinks of marvellous games.
He mends what comes apart.

Though when he isn't here
I can't recall his face,
I'm always glancing at
That slightly freckled space.

His name's quite ordinary
But seems unusual.
His brain's stocked like a shop.
His talk is comical.

Often with other friends
Play ends in biffs and screams:
With him, play calmly goes
Through dusk — and even dreams.

Roy Fuller

My Playmate

I often wonder how it is
   That on a rainy day,
A little boy, just like myself,
   Comes out with me to play.

And we step in all the puddles
   When walking into town,
But though I stand the right way up,
   He's always upside down.

I have to tread upon his feet,
   Which is a sorry sight,
With my right foot on his left foot,
   My left foot on his right.

I really wish he'd talk to me,
   He seems so very kind
For when I look and smile at him
   He does the same, I find.

But I never hear him speaking,
   So surely he must be
In some strange land the other side,
   Just opposite to me.

Mary I. Osborn

47

I Had No Friends At All

I had no friends at all
Until you came my way
And now we play and play
All day. I only hope
You never have to go away.
It would be sad
To lose the only friend
I've ever really had.

John Kitching

Partners

Find a partner,
says sir, and sit
with him or her.
A whisper here,
a shuffle there,
a rush of feet.
One pair,
another pair,
till twenty-four
sit safely on the floor
and all are gone
but one
who stands,
like stone,
and waits;
tall,
still,

alone.

Judith Nicholls

49

Wrestling

I like wrestling with Herbie because
he's my best friend.
We poke each other
(but not very hard)
and punch each other
(but not very hard)
and roll on the grass
and pretend to have fights
just to make our sisters scream.

But sometimes if he hits too much
and it hurts,
I get mad
and I punch him back
as hard as I can
and then we are both crying
and going into our houses
and slamming our back doors on each
   other.

But the next day, if it's sunny,
we come out into our yards
and grin at each other,
and sometimes he gives me an apple
or I give him a cookie and
then we start wrestling again.

Kathleen Fraser

Johnny Bissell

Hey!
Johnny Bissell,
Johnny Bissell,
He can wink,
He can whistle,
He got muscle,
He can tussle,
Get you flat on your back!

Hey!
Johnny Bissell,
Johnny Bissell,
He got hair like a thistle,
He got secrets,
He got dens,
If you're one of his friends.

Hey!
Johnny Bissell,
Johnny Bissell,
Sharp as nails,
Tough as gristle,
Stringy tall,
Heads a ball,
BMX-er
Jumps the stream,
Like a dream,
He can glide.
What a ride!
Hey! Johnny Bissell,
Can I be on your side?

Jamila Gavin

Everybody and Me

Alicia ties shoelaces,
Lee unfastens knots,
Clever Trevor's
liquid paper
covers up your blots.

Pauline forges notes
to get you out of games;
Thugger will thump
any nuisance who
calls you nasty names.

Mike and Neville
know the answers
to sums that might seem hard;
Nicky will fetch balls back
from behind the builders' yard.

Joan will catch a spider
if it hides inside your hood;
Stella can find wellies
when you think
they're lost for good.

If your best friend
has left you, Jane
will walk about with you
and share exciting secrets
with her and Jill and Sue.

Daniel draws dinosaurs
which you can colour in
with felt tip pens
or pencils, from
Stanley's crayon tin.

Podge eats
spare rice puddings,
can manage two or three;
Julia hates sausages,
will give you hers for free.

Jim blows up dead footballs,
fixes them with tape;
Barbara can blow
bubble gum
into amazing shapes.

Ollie and Meg sing Beatles tunes,
tell you all the words,
Gaz will show you
his stamp album,
Jeremy swaps cards,

and if your tooth is wobbly
you can have it pulled by me;
we're twenty-four
very good friends
all of us in 2G!

Irene Rawnsley

The Library Lady

The library lady
Has grey hair
Like grandma's.
She never gets cross.
Once I spilled
Orange juice
All over the cover
Of my book.
When I told her,
She just said,
'Never mind.
Try not to do it again.'
When I was ill,
I was late
Taking my books back.
She just said,
'Where were you last week?
I missed you.
Are you better now?'

The library lady
Helps me to find
The books I like.
She knows
All the exciting stories
And the scary ones.

When I grow up
I'd like to work
In a library.

John Foster

A Good Play

We built a ship upon the stairs
All made of the back-bedroom chairs,
And filled it full of sofa pillows
To go a-sailing on the billows.

We took a saw and several nails,
And water in the nursery pails;
And Tom said, 'Let us also take
An apple and a slice of cake';
Which was enough for Tom and me
To go a-sailing on, till tea.

We sailed along for days and days,
And had the very best of plays;
But Tom fell out and hurt his knee,
So there was no one left but me.

Robert Louis Stevenson

Big-Head

My best friend is brainy;
A genius, no less.
Everything my best friend does
Turns out a big success.

My best friend's athletic;
Good-looking as can be;
And my best friend has perfect taste —
For my best friend is *ME*.

Hazel Townson

Index of First Lines

Alicia ties shoelaces   54
Every time we have painting   42
Find a partner   49
Hayley is a nice person   32
He was a rat, and she was a rat   9
He's breaking that voice in for somebody else   39
Hey!   52
Hey Jinny, ho Jinny   22
I fear it's very wrong of me   18
I had a fight with a boy   14
I had no friends at all   48
I have a friend   44
I have a secret friend   46
I know what *I* feel like   25
I like Anne   30
I like wrestling with Herbie because   50
I'm only little   10
I often wonder how it is   47
I sleep in a room at the top of the house   38
I thought you were my friend   36
It's Susan I talk to not Tracey   8
I went back after a cold   28
Jean get licks in school today   13
John used to be all right   26
Johnny Johnson thinks he can run   14
Lips are for speaking   6
My best friend is brainy   30
My best friend's name is Billy   7
My friend and I   23
My friend Dee   37
Pussy can sit by the fire and sing   16
Sally won't you walk with me   21
The library lady   57
The people who live on the right of us   20
There's good mates and bad mates   12
The tyres on my bike are flat   19
Tracy Venables thinks she's great   31

61

We built a ship upon the stairs   58
When we look in the mirror   40
When you're unkind   33
Who's your pal?   34

Acknowledgements

The Publishers and author would like to thank the following for their kind permission to reproduce copyright material in this book:

Macmillan, London and Baskingstoke for 'Let's Talk' from *Song of the Surreys* by Telcine Turner; Deborah Rogers Ltd Literary Agency for 'Best Friends' by Adrian Henri from *The Phantom Lollipop Lady*, published by Methuen Children's Books Ltd, and for 'Write a Poem about a Friend' by Brian Morse; A.D. Peters & Co. Ltd for 'Friendship Poem' by Roger McGough from *Sky in the Pie*, published by Kestrel Books; Bogle I'Ouverture Publications Ltd for 'Confusion' by Odette Thomas from *Rain Falling Sun Shining*; David Higham Associates Ltd for 'Friends' by Elizabeth Jennings from *The Secret Brother* published by Macmillan, and for 'Mirror Friends' and 'Johnny Bissell' by Jamila Gavin; Raymond Wilson for 'My Best Friend'; Dobson Books Ltd for 'Neighbours' and 'Good Company' by Leonard Clark from *Collected Poems and Verses* for Children; Jean Kenward for 'Marbles' and 'Pictures'; Wes Magee for 'The Classroom Circle' and 'Friends'; Walker Books Ltd for 'Tracy Venables' by Colin McNaughton from *There's an Awful Lot of Weirdos in Our Neighbourhood* © 1987 Colin McNaughton; Dave Calder for 'Just Between You and Me' © Dave Calder 1988; Maggie Holmes for 'I Want'; Dave Ward for 'My Friend Dee'; Irene Rawnsley for 'Copycat' from *Ask a Silly Question*, published by Methuen 1988 and for 'Everybody and Me'; Roy Fuller for 'A Boy's Friend', from his book *Seen Grandpa Lately?*; John Kitching for 'I Had no Friends at all' from *A Very First Poetry Book* (edited by John Foster), published by Oxford University Press; The Society for Promoting Christian Knowledge and Mary Osborn for 'My Playmate' by Mary Osborn from *The Book of a Thousand Poems* published by Evans; Faber & Faber Ltd for 'Partners' from *Midnight Forest* by Judith Nicholls; John Foster for 'The Library Lady' by John Foster

63